Dartmoor Breakouts!
Best Escape Stories

Trevor James

'Big Frank' Mitchell – the 'Mad Axeman'.

(Photo by courtesy of 'Daily Mirror Newspapers')

AUTHOR'S PREFACE

The first convict prisoners arrived at Dartmoor on 2nd November 1850. Within a fortnight the first escape occurred when three men absconded, and it's been going on ever since. An escape-proof prison has not yet been built and probably never will be. The design and remote locations of the most secure jails in the world have failed to match the ingenuity of their inmates, who have overcome seemingly impossible obstacles and escaped.

The history of Dartmoor Prison has a liberal sprinkling of escape stories, some of them more exciting than any work of fiction and so daringly executed even the authorities had a grudging admiration for the boldness and bravery of the prisoners involved in them. Sadly, many men have sought, and found, the most certain method of escape – suicide. It still happens. Others have involuntarily 'escaped' into insanity.

Members of the public are often confused about the meaning of the varous categories of prisoners. There are four categories: A, B, C, and D, each of which is directly related to an individual's escape potential:-

Category A. Those who have the support and the means (possibly on the outside) for escape, or represent a threat to the public. These prisoners are confined in 'high security' prisons.
Category B. High escape risk but do not have the means.
Category C. Not a high escape or security risk, but may be 'opportunists'.
Category D. Represent no risk whatsoever either of escaping or being a threat to the public.

The last two categories of prisoners are confined in Dartmoor Prison today.

Apart from the gangster types held at Dartmoor in the past, whose motives for escape were far from sentimental, most escapees have a domestic problem – jealousy or concern about a wife or girl friend. In the past a prisoner could clear his debts to other inmates by escaping or attempting to escape. An example of this happened some years ago at Channings Wood Prison near Newton Abbot when an inmate successfully absconded and when he was clear of the prison calmly waited by the roadside for a lift back! A prison officer on his way to work kindly obliged. Then there are the 'opportunists' who see a chance to escape and take it there and then. Once they're out though they are often at a loss as to what to do. One man who ran away from the prison farm in 1995 was recognised and apprehended by an off-duty officer in Tavistock who saw him aimlessly walking the streets looking in shop windows.

What happens to recaptured prisoners? When Dartmoor was a War Prison (1809–1815) French and American escapees were locked up for ten days in a large outside stone cell, called the Cachot, without heating or bedding and on two thirds of their normal rations. If the military guards aided their escape those concerned faced a Court Martial and were sometimes shot; a flogging was the mildest punishment they could expect. A civilian helping an escapee got a public whipping, a term in the pillory, or transportation; apprehending an escapee brought a £5 reward and this practice continued well into the 20th century.

In the Victorian convict era a recaptured prisoner was punished by being placed in heavy chains and/or on a restricted diet. Today they are transferred at once to a Category B prison – most likely Exeter. Very close supervision is applied including daily cell checks; compulsory wearing of distinctive green and yellow clothing; transfer to another cell every 28 days; not permitted a ground floor cell or one adjacent to another E list prisoner; every movable item is taken away at 'lock up time'. Normal conditions are restored only when they are no longer considered an escape risk. Loss of remission for escaping or attempting to escape is decided upon by an Independent Judiciary, usually a Judge.

Of the scores of prisoners who have gone 'over the wall' since Dartmoor admitted the first prisoners in 1809 some have been killed in the attempt; most of them were recaptured; all of them found the wide and lonely moor their most formidable guardian.

THE FRENCH AT DARTMOOR

Every prison has a high wall around it and Dartmoor had two such walls when it opened as a French Prisoner of War Depot in 1809. The inner wall had platforms for the soldier guards who kept watch over the interior and who didn't hesitate to shoot or bayonet anyone trying to escape. Most of the prisoners in those early days were sailors, among them crews of privateers, often vicious desperadoes who would stop at nothing in an effort to escape. Under cover of darkness, mist, or heavy rain, many a man, sometimes groups of men, found a way of scaling the boundary walls undetected. This was an achievement in itself, because there were wires strung around the walls with bells suspended from them. If the wire was disturbed, the jangling of the bells was the signal for Drummers to beat 'To Arms!'. Then every guard, on or off duty, armed himself and rushed to apprehend the escapees. The ruthlessness with which this was done is illustrated in the following incident.

In 1810 the Nottinghamshire Militia arrived at Dartmoor and several

Dartmoor Prison 1810 showing the double outer walls
(Author's collection)

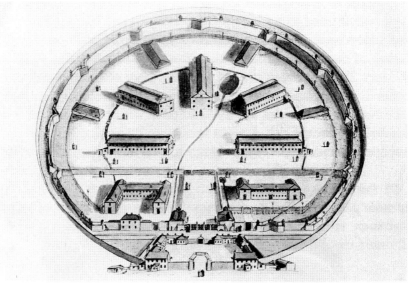

French prisoners, seeking to take advantage of the new arrival's supposed lack of vigilance on their first night on guard duty, attempted a mass escape, but were detected milling about in the area between the two walls known as the 'Military Walk'. When the alarm was given, every Militiaman, some half-clothed, ran to the scene, and in the confusion one of their own men, who hadn't had time to put on his uniform and was mistaken for a prisoner, was stabbed to death by bayonet thrusts.

A Dartmoor prisoner of war attempting to escape not only had the stone walls, alarm bells, and armed sentries to contend with. There was the moor to cross, without signposts, and a population ranged against him, either for fear of punishment if they helped him, or the possibility of a £5 reward if they turned him in. The tors and bogs made travel difficult and there was little shelter; besides, a man needed rest, food, and the means of crossing the Channel. Torbay was usually their objective, where there was a chance of stealing a boat, or maybe persuading a fisherman to take them to France (fishermen on both sides were, by mutual agreement, immune from hostilities during the French wars). Occasionally boats and their occupants were 'hijacked' and forced to sail to France under threat of death. Eventually things got so bad the Admiralty ordered all unattended vessels on the south coast to have their oars and sails removed as a precaution against theft by escaping prisoners of war.

Smugglers were involved in the escape trade, and 'trade' is precisely what developed when professional 'escape agents' began to appear. These men were unscrupulous scallywags who would arrange everything for an escapee - for a price. Lucky customers were whisked away to somewhere safe, perhaps an isolated house or a quiet inn with an understanding (and equally expensive) landlord who would arrange transportation to France. Sometimes things could go tragically wrong though. On 26th January 1811 five French officers living on Parole at Moretonhampstead stole away from their lodgings after dark and met a local Carrier called Richard Tapper who had horses waiting to take them to Topsham on the River Exe near Exeter. There they were joined by two well known smugglers from Cheriton Bishop, brothers Thomas and William Vinnicombe, who, for a down payment of £25 and the promise of another £250, took them on board their boat and set sail down the river for France. At the mouth of the river their luck ran out when the vessel ran aground off Exmouth and they were caught. The French officers, three of whom were ship's captains, were sent to Plymouth, probably to Mill Prison. Tapper and the Vinnicombes were tried at the Devon Assizes in the summer of 1812 and sentenced to transportation for life.

At Dartmoor a number of prisoners were employed outside the prison on road making and various building projects that included the Church and Parsonage. They were paid sixpence a day, but, as reported by the Americans who took over when the French war ended, payment was made every three months and not at all if there was an escape during that period. That didn't stop determined men. One bold Frenchman effected a unique method of escape when his colleagues encased him in a recess in the chimney they were constructing in the Parsonage and walled him in, leaving air holes in loose mortar, and successfully concealing his absence at roll call. The prisoner waited until they departed at the end of the day, forced his way out (the mortar not having had time to set) and made his getaway. The question might be asked: what motivated his companions, knowing they faced certain punishment when he was found to be missing?

As already mentioned, heavy penalties were inflicted on sentries who aided escapees. In addition, a barrier of iron railings inside the inner wall prevented prisoners from approaching the guards and fraternising with them, and maybe bribing them for help in escaping. It did no good because several instances of bribery came to light as well as an unknown number that didn't. In 1812 three French prisoners paid a Roscommons Militiaman £2, the going rate at the time, to help them 'over the wall'. Paddy wasn't the only one among the rank and file who had no scruples about supplementing his pay in this manner. Soldiers were poorly paid and conscripted from the lowest classes, drunkards almost to a man, so it was no surprise to find so many of them willing to risk a flogging, or perhaps their lives, for the price of a drink. There was a sting in the tail though; the Irishman was detected trying to pass forged notes, the price of his treachery, at the daily market that was held within the prison. Forgery was a big problem in every prisoner of war depot and the death penalty had been introduced to try and stop it. The forger, a prisoner called Lustique, was later identified and both he and the soldier were tried and hanged.

On a lighter note, the best known story is that of *Le Capitaine Calonne et sa Dame* – the title of a play performed by the prisoners. Theatricals were a prominent feature of prison life and performances were often attended by the British. On this occasion a certain officer and his wife generously offered to help by lending the leading actors a uniform and female clothing. The offer was gladly accepted and the performance was a huge success until, towards the end, an announcement was made: 'Messieurs, the Captain and his wife have left the prison'. The implication was clear and only too true – the French 'Captain and his wife' had passed unchallenged out of the main prison entrance to freedom, leaving an embarrassed officer and his lady having to endure hoots and whistles of derision from a delighted prisoner audience!

THE AMERICAN MASTER PLAN

In April 1813 the French prisoners at Dartmoor were joined by 250 Americans, mostly sailors captured during the War of 1812 (Britain was fighting two wars at once at this time). When the war with Napoleon ended in April 1814, the French were repatriated, and all American POWs in England were transferred to Dartmoor (except the officers who were on parole). They lost no time in planning to escape, and there are several recorded instances where, like the French, they either fooled or bribed the guards or simply made a run for it. The following is an account of a carefully planned, coordinated, effort that would have had spectacular results had it succeeded.

In August 1814 the American prisoners formulated a master escape plan to tunnel their way out under the prison walls. This was to be the most ambitious attempt at a mass breakout ever devised by prisoners on the 'moor'. They had the place to themselves now the French had gone. They had previously been confined to the north side of the compound, now they were permitted to make use of No. 6 block to ease the congestion, and as more prisoners arrived, they too went to No. 6. This is where the digging began.

Secrecy was vital of course. Bibles were procured and every man involved swore on oath not to reveal by word or sign what was going on; the penalty for treachery was to be death by hanging, a sentence they themselves would carry out. The overcrowding in No. 4 block (which was inside a separate walled-off area) was to be eased by moving men to No. 6, so it was decided to extend the plan to include tunnelling from No. 4 as well. Then the unoccupied No. 5 block was included in the plan. Thus there were three tunnels, running parallel from the central walled compound towards the Two Bridges Road, being excavated at once, and their feeling was that should any tunnel be discovered the chances were at least one would remain undetected.

In *A Prisoner's Memoires*, a book written by an American prisoner called Charles Andrews, published in America after the war, they claim to have sunk shafts 20ft. deep before digging outwards horizontally in an easterly direction. They found the subterranean soil to be light and relatively free of stones, so progress was good. The entrances were very narrow but underground the holes were wide enough for four men to work abreast, and they rigged lamps in a way that induced a circulation of air, stale air being expelled as fresh air entered. The biggest problem was disposing of the excavated material. At first pocketfuls of earth were scattered over the yards, but a more effective way had to be found if progress was to be maintained. The bulk of the dirt was thrown into the fast flowing foul water outlets and an ingenious method was devised for getting rid of the remainder. The prisons were built of roughly dressed 'moor stone' which left large crevices in the walls. The Americans mixed the sandy soil they brought up into a rough mortar and filled in the cracks with it, disguising their work by whitewashing over it. The prison officials afterwards expressed amazement at the amount of material that must have been dug out and never understood how it was disposed of.

By the end of August they had progressed over 60ft. in each tunnel. Then disaster struck when, on 2nd. September, the authorities began a search of No. 5 and 6 blocks. They found one of the entrances, but only after tapping the floors with crowbars, so cleverly was it concealed. All of the prisoners were sent back to occupy No. 1, 2, and 3 blocks and the tunnel was sealed off with stones. (In 1881, during excavations to lay the foundations for a new convict prison, the tunnel was uncovered and found to be 14ft. deep, not 20ft. as the Americans had claimed. An enterprising convict who later occupied a cell directly over the tunnel tried to escape by digging down into it, only to find it was still full of stones.)

Had they been betrayed? An enquiry was held amongst themselves and several prisoners were interrogated on suspicion of turning traitor, but the evidence was inconclusive and it was supposed that careless talk had alerted the authorities. The (segregated) No. 4 prison not having been searched, work there recommenced at once. In September more prisoners began arriving and No.s 5, 6, and 7 blocks had to be made available again to accommodate them. Excavations were immediately resumed and No. 6 tunnel was reopened by men digging around the blockages to reach the old workings. The task was again coordinated with the intention of completing all three tunnels simultaneously, when hundreds of men would pass through them and make their way to the coast. The mass escape was planned for 10.00 pm one stormy night, which would allow time for them to reach the Torbay area before daylight. The men were elated, working eagerly, and confident of success.

Then there was a betrayal when one of their number approached the guards and went off with them, never to be seen again. It was thought he had been repatriated as a reward for his treachery. Once more every man was sent back to the north side of the prison, regardless of overcrowding, whilst repairs were made and the tunnels blocked up. The Americans were placed on two/thirds rations for ten days, the remaining one/third being retained to cover the cost of the work. It was devastating blow for them, and Andrews wrote, 'if the villain had been caught, they should scarcely have tried him but would have torn him to atoms before the life could have time to leave his traitorous body'.

Until the very day of their release the 'Yankees' were bitter enemies, causing unrest and exasperating their captors to the extent one British officer openly proclaimed he would sooner deal with 10,000 Frenchmen than 4,000 American prisoners. Had their tunnels gone undetected many hundreds of them would have been at large and the prison officials would have had to face a problem of unprecedented magnitude - with a headache to match!

RUBBER BONES WEBB

One of the most remarkable and widely remembered escapes from Dartmoor prison since World War II was that of Harold Roy Webb, better known as 'Rubber Bones'. Despite the fact he was doing time for robbery with violence a cavalier spirit surrounds his exploits. For example he once said to a prison officer escorting him 'we don't need these do we?' handing over his handcuffs after slipping his hands free – it was the sort of thing that earned him his nickname as well as his ability to squeeze his supple body through seemingly impossible apertures. The latter feat, as we shall see, was to gain him immortal fame in the history of Dartmoor.

Webb, a native of Northwich, Cheshire, was sentenced at the Old Bailey in October 1946 to eight years imprisonment and ten strokes of the birch for robbery with violence. He already had a record as an Army deserter and had escaped from military custody more than once. It is perplexing therefore to learn that when he was transferred from Wormwood Scrubs to Dartmoor in June 1947 with twenty-four other prisoners, he was the only one in the group who was not manacled to another man like the rest. When they disembarked from the train at Tavistock North Station to board a bus to take them to Princetown he wriggled free of his handcuffs and sprinted away leaving his escorts to ensure the other men were safely accounted for. A passer by some distance away, unaware of the situation, noticed a man climbing a tree and wondered what was going on. It was almost certainly Webb hiding from pursuit until the heat was off.

It took three days to track him down in the worst June weather imaginable – cold and windy with torrents of rain. He was recaptured late one evening near Meldon Quarry, just outside Okehampton almost twelve miles from Tavistock. Webb was a pitiable sight, soaking wet and chilled to the bone, dishevelled and starving. He had survived on berries, spring onions and the tops of broad beans filched from people's gardens. 'I'm the man you are looking for' he mumbled to the policemen who apprehended him. They were convinced he was a dying man.

Dartmoor Prison's forbidding grey walls – Webb occupied a cell in the bottom row of the larger block above the hot air heating system at ground level. The air intakes from which he escaped (now bricked up!) can be clearly seen (Author's collection)

With his previous escape record and the more recent escapade to take into consideration he was placed under extra surveillance when he was taken to Dartmoor, in keeping with the rules set out for the E List prisoners (see author's preface). Yet he accomplished another escape which was to cause a sensation. This time he left by a tunnel, not one he had to dig himself but a man-made one that conducted hot air from the (now obsolete) heating system to each cell. Webb's cell was on the ground floor directly above one of the main ducts. It was during a period employed in the Works Department assisting with repairs that he gained the knowledge he was to use for his escape.

His plan and preparations were a masterpiece of cunning, tenacity and, it must be said, sheer guts. His cell was regularly 'turned over' (minutely searched) and at night an officer looked through the 'Judas Hole' of his cell door every half hour. These were just two of the extra precautions taken under E List rules. Imagine if you can the mixture of shock and disbelief when officers entered is cell on the morning of 20th November 1951 and found an improvised 'dummy' under his blankets and no sign of the occupant! Sometime in the night Webb uncovered the entrance he had made to the ventilation and heating shaft for his cell and squirmed his way down to the warm air ducts below. The fresh air intakes, which were flush with the outer wall of the building at ground level, were fitted with bars and on examination it was apparent the fugitive had used a hacksaw saw to weaken them before prising them open. A discarded ladder, a missing pair of gum boots and overalls were further proof he had left the prison.

How on earth was it done? To this day some of the details are unclear but the tale about Webb being inspired by the famous 'Wooden Horse' escape from a prisoner of war camp, related to Dartmoor inmates only two days previously by a visiting speaker, can be discounted. His cell was situated on the ground floor of D Wing and the concrete floor had a layer of tarmac which he was permitted to keep polished with black wax. In their excellent book The *Truth About Dartmoor*, two ex-prisoners who were there at the time and knew Webb allege he worked for several months using a stolen chisel and screwdriver to pick away at the floor bit by bit and covering his tracks with thick layers of wax polish. It must have taken weeks to break through the concrete floor and then through the brick wall to the warm air supply duct for his cell (the air entered each cell via a grill which for obvious reasons could not be interfered with). The excavated material was disposed of little by little in the prison yards during exercise periods. The aperture through which he went each night to continue working was covered early each morning by a drawing board he had trimmed carefully so it was an exact fit; the cracks were then filled with wax polish as before. Because of the regular checks made by officers he could only work for a few minutes at a time, so Webb's perseverance and determination were of a rare order.

The time came when he entered the main ducts which directed hot air straight from the furnaces to the various parts of the prison. A visit to these underground tunnels today reveal a complicated system of low passageways, treacherous six foot deep wells, and cloister-like arches which connect to other ducts; it is a dangerous and confusing area to be in even with torches to light your way. The whole complex is covered with layers of choking dust which induces violent coughing if disturbed. Imagine going into such a place alone in complete darkness with the sonorous roar of the furnaces and fans blowing searing hot dust-laden air in your face. How to grope your way through this nightmare maze and locate the intakes, then remember the way to and fro', defies the imagination. 'Rubber Bones' Webb did it, to the admiration of his fellow inmates and not a few of the 'screws'.

By the time his absence was reported he was miles away, having located the railway (the now defunct Plymouth – Waterloo main line) and followed it to the little wayside station at Brentor, arriving just in time to board the early morning 'workman train' to Exeter. Every risky endeavour requires a lot of luck to succeed and 'Rubber Bones' enjoyed more than his share of luck that day. Mr 'Jimmy' Osborne, station master, ticket collector, signalman and clerk ran Brentor station single-handed and knew every regular passenger by sight and most of them by name. He was on holiday otherwise the game would have ended there and then for Webb. Then there was the guard to contend with but dressed as he was in overalls and gumboots he mingled with the workmen and was allowed to board without a ticket and without question saying 'I'm working up the line', giving the impression he belonged to the gang of railwaymen and quarry workers already on the train The regular guard too was on leave and the one on the train that day was a temporary replacement – how lucky can you get?

As the train neared Exeter Webb jumped off and continued his journey by road, hitching lifts to London. On arrival however it dawned on him that having accomplished an exceptional feat of daring and endurance his predicament now was precarious to say the least. In short he had no friends in the city who could help him and he had nowhere to go for food and shelter. He never considered going to his home in Northwich because he knew it would be under police surveillance day and night. For the same reason he didn't consider going to Cardiff where his girl friend lived and who was also being watched. Probably in desperation he had risked asking for help at an address in Hackney, letting slip that he was an escapee from Dartmoor Prison.

Scotland Yard soon got hold of this information and accordingly the hunt for him was called off in Devon and concentrated in the capital. With the newspapers keeping track of latest developments and a national hue and cry out for him he wandered around London unrecognized for a week, living rough and sleeping under the barrows left overnight by the 'barrow boys' in a cul-de-sac known as John Bull Yard but which was in fact the rear of 151 Oxford Street. His food consisted of left over fruit and vegetables, some of it rotten and his bed was the hard packed freezing cold ground in the yard.

It was in these dismal surroundings the saga ended. A plain clothes policeman happened to spot Webb as he entered the yard on Saturday 25th November and recognized him. Within minutes a team of C.I.D. men arrived. When challenged Webb gave up without a struggle saying 'I'm glad it's all over'. The ordeal had taken its toll and it showed in his gaunt unshaven features to the extent few people would have recognized him from the description or photos of him that were circulated.

Thus ended one of the biggest manhunts ever launched with more than 8,000 police officers involved altogether. When he was recaptured he had been on the run for five days, short of food and money, sleeping in the open without adequate clothing, and undergoing who knows what stress wondering how much longer he could remain at large before being retaken. The policemen took him to Savile Row and gave him his first hot meal since he left the Moor. After spending the night at Wandsworth Prison he was taken back to Dartmoor where, sad to say, his former admirers now treated him with scorn for giving up so easily (as they thought). As it happened it was not the last prison sentence Webb served nor was it his last escape, but for the rest of his life he was remembered (and still is at Dartmoor) as an exceptionally brave man in his own right.

KEYS

One day in March 1862 a Dartmoor warder on patrol saw a prisoner called Anderson look out from the doorway of his cell. The warder's astonishment could only have been matched by Anderson's dismay. After taking him away to be locked up again the warders carried out a search of his cell and found a skeleton key that had been painstakingly made by the unlucky escapee who happened to pick the wrong moment to look and see if the coast was clear.

Six years previously, on 25th August 1856, it was a warder who was unlucky. Convict James Lake had made a duplicate cell key out of bone salvaged from his meat ration. He fitted it to a piece of stick, put his arm through the ventilation slot adjacent to the door of his iron cell, and managed to insert it into the lock outside. After getting out of his cell he used the key again to liberate another man and together they overpowered the night warder, but their escape attempt was foiled when, during the struggle, the warder's cries alerted his colleagues who were quickly on the scene to apprehend the two convicts and lock them up once more.

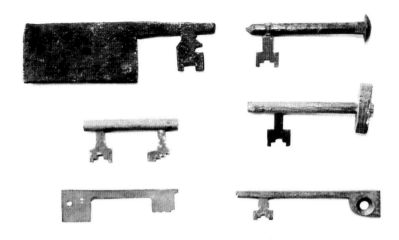

A selection of keys confiscated during routine searches. What use is a key made of cardboard? An inmate trying to escape only needs to use it once! (Courtesy Dartmoor Prison Museum)

Prisoners have been making duplicate keys ever since the convict prison opened and Dartmoor Prison Museum has a collection of them, most of which were confiscated during routine cell searches. The materials used range from wood and bone to plastic and odd scraps of metal. One was fashioned from a toothbrush handle and is still recognisable as such. Many years ago a key was reportedly discovered made from a stiff piece of cardboard.

There are, as you might expect, experts among the prison population to whom most locks present no barrier, which is why prison locks are specially manufactured and guaranteed to be unique in a ratio of several thousand to one. All the same, every lock requires a key and every prisoner is able to observe them several times each day when prison officers lock and unlock cell doors, entrance gates, etc. One man, new to the job, was fumbling with lock and key when a passing inmate cheerfully called 'You've got the wrong key Guv, you want that one!', pointing to another on the bunch.

Would you believe an inmate could make a key out of an odd bit of metal that perfectly matches a prison key, and to a pattern committed to memory, simply by seeing that key in use? It has happened more than once. During training sessions for staff the story is told about a certain prison Governor who habitually waved a key at prisoners when admonishing them. The pattern was memorised and a duplicate was made (and later found). Strict precautions are taken when disposing of unwanted or worn-out keys. At Dartmoor, the pattern is first destroyed by burning with acetylene torches, after which the shanks are buried in concrete to prevent them falling into the wrong hands. The loss of a key or discovery of a duplicate is an extremely serious matter because every lock that key fits has to be changed. In recent years other prisons have had to change hundreds of locks, once, for example, when the imprint of a key was discovered in a piece of pastry hidden in the kitchens, and on another occasion because a duplicate key was found in a cell. On 10th March 1998 the *Daily Mail* reported an incident at Wakefield Prison, Yorkshire, when an inmate was apprehended letting himself back in with a skeleton key. He had unlocked three doors and a gate in the security fence, and it was thought he was making a 'dummy run' in preparation for a planned escape when associates would pick him up. In the same year a cell key was lost at Dartmoor and locks had to be changed.

Modern cells have solid metal doors (although there are still a small number of old style wooden ones at Dartmoor) without a handle or locking mechanism on the inside, so escaping from a cell is a rare occurrence. The risk arises when inmates leaves their cells to go to exercise or to work. On Boxing Day 1966 five Dartmoor prisoners ganged up on their two supervising officers in the gymnasium, tied them up, and stole their keys in order to escape. In his book *The Story of Dartmoor Prison* former Governor Mr. Basil Thomson relates how a warder lost a key in April 1860. A series of escape attempts with a reproduction key took place, and several more were later discovered. 'The trail of the lost key may be traced in the prison records for more than ten years' he wrote. Imagine how often it must have been copied and how many ounces of precious tobacco changed hands among inmates anxious to gain possession of it.

FRANK MITCHELL THE 'MAD AXEMAN'

There was never an escape from prison that caught the public's attention more than that of Frank Mitchell who disappeared from an outside working party in December 1966. It was a typical winter's day on Dartmoor, windy, cold and wet when 'Big Frank' (see title page) literally vanished. Stories about his eventual fate vary, but there can be no doubt he was assisted by London-based criminals and was later murdered for reasons we can only speculate on.

Dartmoor Prison officers remember him as a man who rejoiced in his enormous physical strength and took every opportunity to show it off. A gentle giant with the mind of a child, he would turn into a raging bull of a man in an instant if something upset him; yet in the main he was a trouble-free inmate providing he was tactfully handled. For a big man he wasn't tall, under 6ft. with very broad shoulders and a huge chest; 'stocky' would be an appropriate word to use in describing him. The newspapers dubbed him 'The Mad Axeman' but Frank wasn't 'mad' and wasn't a murderer either. He was certainly a tough and highly dangerous individual who arrived at Dartmoor with a fearsome reputation.

He was born in Kennington in the Borough of Lambeth in 1929, and attended a special school for backward children. He soon became a delinquent and graduated to crime including housebreaking, office breaking, and robbery with violence, all of which earned him terms of imprisonment. An associate of the infamous Kray gang he often helped out on 'The Firm' as they called themselves. In prison he could be an unruly, violent inmate and in two recorded instances corporal punishment was administered.

Pentonville 1954 – 15 strokes with the 'cat o' nine tails' for gross personal violence. He had assaulted three warders:

Hull Prison 1962 – 15 strokes with the birch for attacking two warders.

Because of his bad behaviour and uncontrollable tantrums he was sent to Rampton and later to Broadmoor. He escaped from both institutions and whilst on the run from Broadmoor robbed an elderly couple in their home after threatening them with an axe, thus earning his title, 'The Mad Axeman'. In 1958, at Berkshire Assizes, he was sentenced to life imprisonment for robbery with violence with no fixed date for his release.

At Dartmoor, the last prison he was in, stories about Frank Mitchell are numerous and impressive. One retired prison officer who knew him well said: 'He was a giant of a man, a fitness fanatic who was always exercising in his cell or at work. He would pick up iron bars, boulders, in fact anything to hand and lift them above his head. On one occasion an inmate, a heavily-built man, was injured in the quarry and I was about to send for a stretcher when Mitchell intervened. 'No need for that, Guv.' he said, 'I'll carry him for you'. 'You will never do it' I told him – but he did. I helped get the casualty on his shoulders and he carried him non-stop all the way to the prison and into the hospital, a distance of half a mile or more'. Another officer recalls how Mitchell once lifted two officers at once in a 'bear hug', one under each arm. "It was his idea of being playful, but his regular minders kept out of his way because he'd broken an officer's bones doing that in another prison – he didn't know his own strength" he said. Tales about Frank carrying a 3 cwt. sack of coire from the stores to the mat-making shop and lifting the rear of a Triumph Vitesse police car (parked outside what is now the High Moorland Visitor Centre) with two police officers inside and turning it 180 degrees, are enshrined in Dartmoor's history.

Mitchell's work party were engaged in erecting fences at Bagga Tor, about eight miles from the prison. Lunch was taken in a hut close by and prepared by one of the prisoners from supplies they brought with them. The men who were selected for the 'Honour Parties' as they were called then were generally those with only a short time left to serve and who had good behaviour records (all the more remarkable Mitchell was included). As only one officer was in charge and because some prisoners necessarily worked beyond his field of vision (they were strung out over a two mile long fence) it would have been easy for any one of them to slip away unobserved.

On the afternoon of Monday 12th December 1966 the weather was atrocious on Dartmoor and Mitchell's party took shelter in their hut. Frank left the hut on a pretext and did not reappear. There was no radio communication with the prison in those days and when he failed to turn up for the journey back, the officer in charge raised the alarm by telephoning from a public call box in Peter Tavy, the nearest village. One of the biggest manhunts ever mounted for an escaped Dartmoor prisoner was then organised. The police set up road blocks and officers with tracker dogs searched moorland farms, outhouses, cattle sheds, and barns. They were assisted by soldiers of the Wessex Brigade, Royal Marine Commandos from 41 Commando, Bickleigh, and men of the Argyll and Sutherland Highlanders from Seaton Barracks, Crownhill.

Constable (later Superintendent) D. Roper, the Princetown 'Bobby' making enquiries during the search for Mitchell (Courtesy Simon Dell M.B.E., Q.C.B.)

Prison officers were allocated to search parties looking for the man the Press called 'the most dangerous criminal in England' and a Royal Air Force helicopter from Chivenor, North Devon, was called in to help (the police force did not yet have one).

They were still looking for Mitchell at Christmas. On 29th December a retired prison officer who had known him when he was serving at Broadmoor made a personal appeal to him on nationwide television to give himself up. 'Frank', he said, 'you've made your point, and the sooner you give yourself up the better your case will be... if you wish to approach me I will do all I can to assist you and convey you to the authorities'. It was a wasted effort because by then Frank Mitchell was dead.

On Sunday 11th December, the day before the escape, a big Rover car turned up at the Forest Inn at Hexworthy and three muscular, smartly dressed men had breakfast. In the afternoon two of them were admitted as visitors to Dartmoor Prison, using what were later found to be false names. That evening a garage attendant in Tavistock spoke to them on the forecourt when they asked for a map of the area; when they were told there was not one available, they drove off after receiving directions on how to get to Peter Tavy, near to where Mitchell's party was working. It seems certain they picked up Frank Mitchell by arrangement the next day and by nightfall he was installed in a flat in East Ham, London. When prison clothing with his prison number stamped on it was found a day or two later in a lay-by at Tedburn St. Mary on the old main A 30 road leading out of the county, the search was extended to the London area. Armed police visited the homes of known criminals who might have been harbouring him, but without success.

Meanwhile an embarrassed Home Secretary and a new Dartmoor Prison governor were having to explain several anomalies concerning one of the most sensational episodes in the entire history of the prison. What was a man like Mitchell doing in Dartmoor in the first place? Shouldn't he have been sent back to Broadmoor or similar institution? Why was he permitted to join an outside work party with a history of violence, previous escapes, and an indefinite period still to serve? Why was the advice of senior prison officers not to allow Mitchell outside the prison ignored? These are some of the questions which were asked in the House of Commons by Mr Michael Heseltine, M.P. for Tavistock at that time. As a result, the Committee of Enquiry under Lord Louis Mountbatten, which had been set up to enquire into the circumstances surrounding the escape of the convicted spy George Blake from Wormwood Scrubs in October 1966, was given the additional task of investigating recent events at Dartmoor. A high security fence, floodlighting, the formation of a prison dog section, and (to the prison officers' delight) a radio communication system were among the enquiry's recommendations, all of which were implemented.

'Big Frank' was killed on 23rd December after only eleven days of 'freedom' cooped up in the London flat; no-one was convicted of his murder and his body was never found. The late Ronald Kray, in his book *My Story* (Pan Books) claims he knows who killed Mitchell and names an associate, Billy Exley, who, he says, was paid to take him out of the country with the help of three Greeks and that they murdered him instead. It was Exley who later tipped off the police it was the Krays who did it and later gave evidence for the prosecution at their trial. Whoever was responsible, what did the murderers do with the body? The story is told within the Prison Service that several prisoners, whilst being transferred from one prison to another, have pointed out to their escorts the same concrete pillar supporting a motorway bridge which, they say, is where Mitchell's corpse was disposed of in a mix of concrete. Another account alleges his killers studied the funeral notices in the newspapers and put his body in a ready dug grave late at night, under the lining. The legal occupant was afterwards interred on top and Frank Mitchell was lost to the world for ever.

In 1999 Freddie Foreman, a Kray gang member who had been acquitted on a charge of murdering Frank Mitchell and knew he couldn't be charged twice for the crime, (the law has since been changed) appeared on a television programme entitled *The Krays – Unfinished Business* where he admitted shooting him repeatedly together with a man called Alfie Gerard. The body was allegedly dumped overboard off Newhaven from a boat on a smuggling run to Belgium and France. (See also *Nipper Read – The Man Who Nicked the Krays* by Detective Superintendent Leonard Read and James Morton Little, Brown & Co. 2001).

Two prison Chaplains who made assessments of Mitchell in prison have the last word. One of them strikes an optimistic note after finding him reading poetry in his cell: 'This man has a fund of fearlessness and courage which could, in other circumstances, have made him a very useful citizen'. The second was prophetic and nearer the truth one feels: 'A tough-seeming, but weak, impressionable, young man, fond of posing as the toughest of the boys...there seems almost no hope for his future'.

LOW RISK PRISONERS – CAN YOU EVER BE SURE ?

Category C prisoners are not a high escape or security risk, but may be opportunists. Category D prisoners represent no risk whatsoever either of escaping or being a threat to the public.

Dartmoor Prison farm closed in 2004. With its demise there ended a long history of success when prize cattle, sheep and horses were bred and the enclosed areas of the surrounding moor were transformed into productive farmland. This was a part of the original conditions under which the Duchy of Cornwall leased the land to the prison authorities and it was highly labour-intensive. In recent years the farm proper was a popular workplace with prisoners, the one essential requirement being they had to be Category C or D.

It was October 1973 when the Farm Foreman, Mr. D. Kennelly, took two inmates to do some repair work to the prison leat (a four mile long shallow waterway which at that time extracted water from the River

Walkham to supply the prison). The two men with him were 37 year old Peter Frost (serving six years for burglary) and 29 year old George Peart (also serving six years for theft and forgery). Both men were low category prisoners and they were both due for release within weeks so anyone would have felt safe and at ease in their company.

Mr. Kennelly drove them to their place of work in the prison van and on the way back he decided to check a cowshed on another part of the farm. All three entered the shed where, without warning, the foreman was viciously attacked and overpowered. He was trussed with sisal cord and tape around his ankles and knees; his wrists were also tied behind his back with cord and tape; finally they put a cloth over his head and taped it over his mouth to prevent him calling for help. For good measure they then tied him to a water trough in the shed and left him, making their escape in the van – an Austin 'Gypsy'.

It took Mr. Kennelly two hours of frantic struggling to get free from the trough by which time the escapees had driven to Bishopsteignton, near Teignmouth, and abandoned the van in a copse. The prison had not an inkling that anything was amiss and the fugitives had more than a head start in their flight. On Dartmoor a thick mist with drizzle had descended when, still bound and gagged, their victim managed to roll and crawl across a field to the Rundlestone – Two Bridges road, a remarkable feat for a man who had been savagely beaten and tied up. Sadly three drivers ignored the sight of a man lying helpless at the side of the road but at last two holidaymakers pulled up and freed him. After being taken to the prison by his rescuers and raising the alarm Mr. Kennelly was admitted to the prison hospital for treatment to his wounds.

The abandoned prison van was later discovered by farmer Mr. G. Webber who notified the police. They at once attended the scene with tracker dogs but after several hours lead ahead of their pursuers by the escapees it was a hopeless task to trace them. By now they were almost certainly out of the county but the hunt for them continued relentlessly and they were finally located in London. Frost made no resistance on being arrested. Peart put up a fight when he was located on a building site in the capital but was restrained and both men were returned to Devon to await trial for their misdeeds.

Both men appeared before Mr. Justice Bristow in January 1973 at Bodmin Crown Court on three charges:-

1. Escaping from Dartmoor Prison.
2. Taking a vehicle without consent.
3. Causing bodily harm to Mr. Kennelly.

The only mitigating factor in Frost's case was that he had surrendered peacefully when arrested. Peart on the other hand had strongly resisted arrest. His counsel suggested only sufficient violence had been used in the attack on Mr. Kennelly to ensure an escape and that the attack itself had not been a vicious one! It was in all probability the only mitigating circumstance which could be put forward but it was dismissed by the Judge. Both men had an extra eighteen months added to their existing sentences.

The Farm Foreman was the victim of an 'opportunist' escape and a betrayal of the trust that went with a Category C and D designation. The ruthless handling he received at the hands of these two individuals resulted in him being invalided out of the Prison Service at only thirty years of age.

VIOLENCE, GLAMOUR, AND PUNISHMENTS

Prison escapes have, in the past, often been regarded as some kind of sporting event by members of the public who frequently gave recaptured prisoners an ovation similar to that directed at many television and 'pop' idols today. An extreme case was that of two escaped convicts who were cornered at South Tawton, near Okehampton, in 1851. A farmer and his son assisted the local Constable in capturing them and were badly injured in the struggle, the farmer being severely kicked and beaten. The Constable suffered head injuries after being hit with a stone

Mounted Warders sally forth on a typical misty winter's day on Dartmoor. They kept watch over outside working parties and were called out to search for escapers when the need arose

(Courtesy of Dartmoor Prison Museum)

tied in a handkerchief. All three men then had to fight off the populace, who had sided with the runaways and plied them with tobacco and beer. One of the convicts was quite drunk when he was finally secured. Dartmoor Prison's evil reputation was then in the making, which probably accounted for the inhabitants sympathising with the fugitives.

The Reverend Clifford Rickards in *A Prison Chaplain on Dartmoor* tells how several prisoners got away from a farm party near the prison, only to be recaptured almost at once. They were marched back through Princetown to the prison. Shouts of 'They've got them!' and 'Here they come', attracted the Reverend into the street in time to see a huge crowd of residents and visitors surrounding a group of warders escorting the escapees back to jail. Loud cheering and shouts of encouragement rang out, to the delight of the prisoners who laughed back at them and appeared to be having the time of their lives. Reverend Rickards then relates another side of the story: further up the street a group of anxious women had gathered, all of them warders' wives. 'It's no laughing matter for us', they said, 'it's our husbands who will be made to suffer when the enquiry is made'. And so it was: the warders, who were invariably held responsible for escapes, were fined or demoted for neglect of duty.

A similar, but less 'glamorous' episode, took place in 1879, and the excitement of the chase, together with the subsequent treatment of the recaptured men, was vividly portrayed by a convict who was present at the scene. He described the event in a letter smuggled out of Dartmoor to a prison acquaintance who had completed his sentence. The instigator of the escape attempt was a prisoner named Morgan who had run away once before, and was obviously an 'opportunist' hell-bent on making a getaway. (Taken from *Convict Life* by 'Ticket of Leave Man', Wyman & Sons 1879).

The day's work was done and the farm party had stacked their rakes, forks and other tools before going to collect their hats and coats, which had been left beside a hedge some distance away. 'Now's our chance!' cried Morgan, and eight men disappeared over the hedge in a trice, 'leaving their guards open mouthed and decidedly off their guard. But of their escape there was no fear', the letter said, 'thirty or forty Devonshire labourers had heard the alarm whistle and the signal gun. They were soon joined by others and in strong parties started in pursuit. I think I may safely say that for the reward for each capture there will be at least half a dozen claimants.' (A reward of £5 was payable for apprehending an escapee.)

Meanwhile the rest of the party were marched back to the prison, passing on the way 'an excited, pale-faced youth, flourishing a double-barrelled shotgun in a most alarming manner, exclaiming 'Which way have they gone, who will I shoot?' He has been the butt of a good many jokes since, for it was discovered when the time came to shoot he had left his ammunition pouch at his quarters!'

It being a perfectly clear evening with visibility of at least twenty miles, the fugitives were quickly rounded up. 'Last Friday', the letter went on, 'Director Morrish came down to Dartmoor redolent with the odour of Whitehall and armed with all the majesty of a Supreme Judge. Five of the men received two dozen each with the 'cat' and the other three were birched. I saw the runaways this morning in their yellow dresses (yellow clothing worn by recaptured escapees), they are breaking stones.' As for the warders, the account concludes: 'This morning the Governor received from Parliament Street the decision of the Directors as to the punishment of the officers who were in charge. They are each fined ten shillings and reduced to Probation Class for three months, so their pay will be reduced for that period.'

'JUMBO' PARSONS

In most prisons sooner or later an incident will occur that is not only memorable and unusual but beggars belief for audacity.

Charles 'Jumbo' Parsons, as his nickname suggests, was a big man who stood well over six foot tall and was built like the proverbial barn door. He was also a dangerous and violent criminal who was sentenced to seven years imprisonment for robbery with violence at the Central Criminal Court on 29th January 1957. The proceeds of the robbery were never recovered.

Parsons turned up in Devon with his wife whilst 'on the run', having escaped from another prison. They stayed for just a few days at a time at various caravan sites, trying to keep ahead of the Metropolitan Police 'Flying Squad' who were actively pursuing them. The 'Squad' men were aware their quarry had been known to carry a revolver (a much less common occurrence in the 1950s) and were anxious to put him back behind bars where he could do no harm.

The Parsons' mistake was to have parcels sent 'Care of the G.P.O.' which they collected from the local post offices wherever they happened to be. It is a reasonable assumption that the packages contained money from the proceeds of the robbery with which to fund their escapade. It can also be concluded they had very trustworthy friends or relatives assisting them. In October 1957 the police officers following their trail decided to concentrate on the Torbay area and the numerous caravan sites there, not forgetting the main post office which was kept under continuous surveillance. True to form Mrs. Parsons called to collect a parcel and was followed by the officers to Paignton and thence to a caravan site at Goodrington. Policemen and dog handlers from Torquay and Paignton assembled at 7.00 pm that same day and quietly surrounded the caravan Mrs. Parsons had been seen to enter. They knocked at the door and when it was opened they burst in to find 'Jumbo' with his hat and coat on and his bags packed ready to depart. They were in the nick of time and for Parsons the game was up. He was returned to prison and later transferred to Dartmoor.

A year later, on Monday 13th October 1958, there was a flurry of police activity at Dartmoor when evidence of a planned escape was discovered in the prison quarry. A prison officer found a revolver and a note hidden among some rocks together with a toilet bag which contained money, a rough map of the area, and two driving licences with certificates of insurance. The map indicated a wood known locally as 'Long Plantation' where a car had been left and on investigation a fairly new black Austin A.55 was found with the ignition key in the switch and ample petrol in the tank. It was later established the vehicle bore false number plates and the documents mentioned had been stolen in London days before. Two sports jackets, trousers and a shirt were in the boot. It was obvious an escape was to take place by a prisoner with ample funds and the help of well-paid accomplices and/or loyal family members. This ambitious plan had now been foiled and there must have been much grinding of teeth by a certain Dartmoor Prison inmate, the most likely person being 'Jumbo' Parsons who was in residence on the moor.

The events that took place just seven months later were not only astonishing in their boldness but were similar in several respects to those just related and what is more, were proved to be related to inmate Parsons.

Jan. 1931 and a prisoner escaped over the wall at this point. A plain clothed policeman gives bloodhounds the scent from the escapee's clothing and the hounds followed the scent all the way to Plymouth where the fugitive was apprehended. Farmer with cap assisted search on horseback. The ladies bred bloodhounds and loaned them for such occasions. (Courtesy of Simon Dell M.B.E., Q.C.B.)

At about 2.00 am on the night of 18th May 1959 a Dartmoor Prison officer happened to glance out of the third floor window where he was standing and was flabbergasted when he saw a man in civilian clothing stroll across the prison yard inside the boundary walls. The October 1958 incident was fresh in the minds of every member of staff and the officer therefore wasted no time in contacting the Principal Officer on duty in the Orderly Room who at once organised a search for the intruder. He himself took part and by chance came across a man crouching against a partly demolished wall who immediately ran off shouting 'Get away! Get away!' which was (rightly) interpreted by his pursuer as a warning to partners in crime. The man was caught and was recognised to be Edward Charles Ward who had not only been released from Dartmoor just days before but had occupied a cell in the very prison wing that housed 'Jumbo' Parsons.

Ward admitted breaking into the prison using a discarded scaffold pole to scale the boundary wall and that the purpose of his 'visit' was to bring in a quantity of 'snout' (prison slang for tobacco). It was realised that Ward was almost certainly not alone, having called out repeated warnings whilst being chased and a full alarm was raised. The Princetown Police Constable was informed who in turn would have telephoned Police Headquarters in Exeter. Things then moved quickly as the Deputy Governor supervised a hunt outside the prison for Ward's accomplices. Two men were disturbed in the vicinity of the American Cemetery (the burial ground for American prisoners of war captured in the War of 1812) who fled in the direction of 'Long Plantation' which lies about a mile from the prison in the Two Bridges direction.

The Princetown Constable made his way to 'Long Plantation' where he discovered a Ford Consul motor car with false number plates, afterwards found to have been stolen in Middlesex. The engine was still warm. Meanwhile Detective Sergeant C.J.Tarr arrived from Plympton and after talking with Ward went to the prison yard where he found the scaffold pole with a length of rope attached which had been used to gain entry. The most significant find was a large car jack and a sledge hammer close to the ground floor cell occupied by Parsons. There can be no doubt as to the use these would have been put if Ward had not been detected.

What about the two men who had been seen running away from the Deputy Governor's search party? As part of the police procedures a Motor Patrol Constable was in the vicinity of Moretonhampstead when at 3.20 am he passed a car travelling in the opposite direction towards Exeter. It was a Ford Zodiac containing two men and the police driver's suspicions were at once aroused. Not being able to stop this vehicle he reported the incident and every police force in the westcountry was alerted. The car was intercepted and stopped two hours later on the A30 main road to London near Yeovil. The occupants were two well-known criminals, twenty three year old John William Hayes of Hillingdon, Middlesex and

Benjamin Hiller, thirty three, from Tooting, London. They were taken to Yeovil Police Station and detained for questioning.

Detective Sergeant Tarr travelled up from Devon to interview Hiller and Hayes who admitted having been in the Moretonhampstead area only because they had got lost returning from Torquay. They both denied knowing Ward but a search of the two men, their vehicle and belongings revealed damning evidence to the contrary. When Hayes was searched two car parking tickets and three cinema tickets were found – all originating from Newton Abbot. It was more than likely that Ward was the third man to visit the cinema and had driven the second car, the one found at Long Plantation for the escape. In the Zodiac was a suitcase containing shoes size 10½ and a suit to fit a man more than six feet tall, all intended for 'Jumbo' Parsons no doubt, but how to prove it?

To begin with Hiller said the clothing was his but as he was only 5 foot 8 inches tall and his companion Hayes was even smaller it was obviously untrue and both men were taken back to Devon to be remanded in custody. It was at this point that meticulous examination of the suit was rewarded. Not only was it a perfect fit for Parsons but when the pockets were turned inside out the wallet section in the jacket revealed a tailor's trade tag which was not visible unless the lining was fully exposed. As well as a reference number the tag bore the words '14th April 1956 – C.A.Parsons'. This evidence and enquiries at the (London) tailors, together with recognition of the three men by staff at the Newton Abbot cinema was a crucial part of the total proof with which to charge the three men as follows:-
1.   Jointly and feloniously conveying a sledge hammer, a car jack and rope into H.M.Prison, Dartmoor with intent to facilitate the escape of a prisoner there confined.
2.   Conspiracy. Hayes was further charged with stealing the car from Middlesex.

At Devon Quarter Sessions held on 3rd July 1959 Ward, Hayes and Hiller, all known criminals, were each sentenced to two years imprisonment on both charges, the sentences to run concurrently. Hayes was awarded an additional two years for larceny of the car. Their pal 'Jumbo' Parsons remained in his Dartmoor cell.

THE HUNTERS AND THE HUNTED

The task of searching for escaped prisoners has always rested with the police force. Prison warders worked closely with the police, manning road blocks and assisting in searches as directed by them, but if the escapees were still at large three days later, they were recalled to run the prison and the local constabulary assumed sole responsibility.

Prior to 1966 Dartmoor Prison did not have radio communications, a dog section, or an internal security fence. In addition there was a more dangerous and desperate type of criminal interned there, many of them serving long sentences and therefore highly motivated towards escaping. Nearly every escapee who did abscond did so in the winter when the weather was at its worst or under cover of mist and the long nights. Those engaged in looking for them faced almost unbearable hardships, turning out at a moment's notice (the Tavistock Police abandoned their annual Christmas Dinner on one occasion) to face long hours manning isolated checkpoints or tramping over the moors, perhaps in torrents of rain, sleet, or snow, with icy winds that cut through their uniforms (there was no special protective clothing issued). It was worse for the fugitives, who were even less adequately clad, and unsure of their whereabouts. Policemen long retired have a fund of horror stories about their experiences, some of which would be held in doubt had they been told by someone other than a trusted 'Bobby'.

On one occasion two escapees were found by police cowering in the snow, half-frozen, and actually crying with pain in the cold. Another prisoner, desperate for food, tore the leg off a dead sheep and ate the raw meat; yet another consumed some candles he found in an abandoned farmhouse where he took shelter.

For the hunters there was no shelter. Policemen were posted to lonely crossroads and bridges to maintain a vigil for as long as was necessary, perhaps several days, and were expected to remain there until relieved. These duties were often shared by prison warders, but there were times when the police had to go it alone. One old-timer, Mr. Ken Northey of Tavistock, recalls spending fourteen hours at Moorshop on the edge of Dartmoor, in the dark, in a snowstorm, alone and without refreshment. By morning he was so cold he sought the meagre shelter of the nearest ditch and kept watch from there. He had to face the uncompromising wrath of his Inspector when he turned up next morning. Another policeman was manning a bridge overlooking the railway on the outskirts of Tavistock. After enduring a cold, lonely night, and with snow falling, he was delighted when, in the morning, a baker's van delivering freshly made pasties to Tavistock, stopped and the driver offered him one. When he looked inside he discovered his 'hot fresh pasties' were frozen and

In a story not related here – Major L. Morris, Chief Constable of Devon and former Governor of Dartmoor Prison (centre) took to the skies to search for John Gasken in November 1932 (Courtesy of K. Saunders, author of Devon Aerodromes in Old Photographs*)*

covered in a layer of snow that had penetrated the cracks in the doors. Nevertheless, with commendable determination, a ravenous constable managed to find a palatable pasty at the bottom of the pile.

The popular notion of officers chasing fugitives over the moors in a mist with bloodhounds straining at the leash is only partly true. Neither the prison nor the police had bloodhounds to employ, but there were at least two generous sources from which help came from time to time. In the 1920s a Miss Lowe of Minions, near Liskeard, Cornwall, loaned three hounds to help police and warders hunt down two desperate escapees. They were directed and controlled by a Miss Clarke, and although they were not directly responsible for recapturing the two men, the dogs proved invaluable in guiding search parties all the way from Princetown to Roborough Down in driving wind and rain along the very route they'd taken, as was proved by the discovery of their discarded prison clothing. Both men were later apprehended in Plymouth.

From 1946 until 1953 assistance was freely given by Mrs. H.M. Blakiston of Bratton Tor Kennels, Bratton Clovelly (and later of Lydford) who bred bloodhounds. This lady knew, as did Miss Lowe and Miss Clarke before her, that hounds only worked to advantage under the direction of their owners; consequently she accompanied the police on many occasions, sometimes across rough country, often at night and in bad weather. A former traffic policeman, Mr. R. Borlase, recalls sending a car to Bratton Clovelly to collect bloodhounds and the resident Constable, the late Mr. J. Gater, immediately the force was informed a prisoner was at large. P.C. Gater got to know the dogs well and became proficient in handling them himself, especially a hound named 'Turpin'. Mrs. Blakiston had paid seventy-five guineas for him and trained him herself specially for tracking.

It was P.C. Joe Gater who, with P.C. Brian Kendrick, was responsible for forming the Devon Constabulary dog unit in the late 1950s, based in Torquay. In 1964, the unit was extended to other stations, including Tavistock. They used Alsatians who could not only track, but were capable of apprehending an escapee until their handlers caught up with them. Dartmoor Prison followed suit on the recommendation of the Mountbatten Enquiry after Frank Mitchell's escape in 1966. Police dogs, with their handlers, manned the prison for several months to enable prison officers and dogs to be trained. The prison dog section today plays a prominent role in drugs detection with its sniffer dogs.

For more than sixty years the Devon Police have worked to guidelines set out in an 'Escape Scheme' devised by a remarkable man, Major Lyndon Henry Morris, C.B.E., M.C., D.L. He was the Governor of Dartmoor Prison (the youngest ever to hold that position) prior to taking up the post of Chief Constable of Devon on 2nd April 1931 He was therefore well qualified to organise a system that has been successful for so long and with amendments, is still in use today. For security reasons the details cannot be revealed except to say the plan involved sealing off the moor, setting up roadside check points, and directing search parties from a Central Control Room. Police helicopters are an essential part of every escape operation today.

A convict hunt used to be the only occasion when policemen could claim overtime, after all available resources and the Special Constabulary had been mobilised. The 'Specials' were, and are, a voluntary force, but no less enthusiastic for that. The author remembers one Special Constable – his father-in-law, the late Mr. EJ. Batten of Brentor – spending many a cold winter night keeping watch on the railway lines at Brentor station, turning out after working all day and going to work as usual the next day. 'Rubber Bones' Webb, boarded a train at Brentor station and got clear of the county. By tradition the policeman who actually caught an escaped prisoner had the privilege of returning him to Dartmoor and on at least one occasion it was a 'Special' who did the honours.

One might think that after all the inconveniences and privations endured in order to capture them, prisoners would receive little sympathy from their captors. In fact the opposite has been the case. The pitiful condition some escapees have been found in has aroused the finest instincts in the policemen involved, who are on record as having had a 'whip-round' at the station to nip along to the nearest cafe or fish and chip shop to buy a hot meal for a starving prisoner. Others have been plied with sandwiches and endless mugs of tea whilst cheerful banter was often exchanged in the aftermath of a successful 'hunt'. I quote the words of an 'old lag' ('Rubber Bones', writing in The *People* Sunday newspaper after his release from prison) who was recaptured near Okehampton wet through, starving, and exhausted, after three days on the run in freezing November weather:

"After my capture kind arms took hold of me, the arms of the Devon Constabulary. 'Poor devil' said one. 'He must be nearly dead' said another. Then I found a paper bag full of cakes in one hand and an orange in the other, whilst a cigarette was being thrust in my mouth and someone else was lighting it. I'll never forget those grand, fine policemen." After describing being taken to Tavistock police station, he concluded: "I did not stay long in that dream world. Very soon two warders arrived from Dartmoor prison." All of which sums up very well the usual conclusion to a Dartmoor escape.

THE CAPTURE OF 'RUBY' SPARKS

What was one of the most astonishing convict related incidents of all time happened in London in 1940. Among Dartmoor Prison's most notorious inmates was John Charles 'Ruby' Sparks, a well known criminal specialising in 'smash and grab' robberies and burglary. Army deserter and ringleader in Dartmoor's famous mutiny in 1932, Sparks escaped from the moorland jail in January 1940 and was at large for 170 days – an all-time record made possible largely by the wartime 'blackout'. In August that year he was traced to an address in North London and four 'Flying Squad' detectives went there and arrested him. At the Station their suspect (naturally) protested his innocence and persisted in wearing the dark glasses he had on when apprehended. The Squad men had a problem because they had acted on information received without any direct evidence with which to charge him or indeed take his fingerprints. Everything hinged on getting Sparks to admit his true identity.

Three of the team knew Sparks but could not be certain they had their man. The fourth man was Detective Sergeant Matthew Brinnand, only recently promoted and retained on the Squad (the usual practice was to be transferred after being promoted). He was obviously highly thought of by his commanding officers and their confidence in him was about to be justified in a remarkable manner. His three colleagues who were acquainted with Sparks debated for a quarter of an hour and decided they had to let him go. Brinnand disagreed and said if he was released he personally would arrest him the moment he set foot outside. There was an argument lasting another ten minutes but Brinnand was adamant. 'That man is Sparks!' he declared 'let him go if you want but if you do I will arrest him on the pavement outside'.

The detainee listened to all this with mounting anger and finally lost his composure, smashing his dark glasses on the floor and cursing Det. Sgt. Brinnand. Thus ended the most lengthy escape by a prisoner from Dartmoor Prison. Did Matthew Brinnand have a 'gut feeling' about Sparks or was it a clever ploy designed to make their man lose his temper the way he did and admit his identity? Whichever it was the fugitive realised the game was up and it had all been for nothing – the sequel to practically every escape attempt on record.

Footnote

This remarkable man was a mixture of good and bad. During the 1932 mutiny at Dartmoor Prison, Sparks saved a warder from assault and possibly being murdered. When World War II broke out he volunteered for the British Army but during a forty-eight hour leave period got into trouble over forged ration books. At his trial his Commanding Officer gave a character reference for him saying he was a fine soldier and didn't want to lose him. It did no good and 'Ruby' was sent back to Dartmoor. Like so many others he took a wrong path in life otherwise he might have been a credit to society.

A WINTER'S TALE

What former Dartmoor Prison Governor Basil Thomson called 'a sensational escape' occurred on 2nd January 1898. It involved convict William Morgan who had previously escaped from Parkhurst on the Isle of Wight before being transferred to Dartmoor. Perhaps because of this he was allocated a cell in one of the recently constructed 'modern' blocks which were considered to be escape proof. In those days only the ground floor cells had bars fitted to the windows, but they all had cast iron frames with panes a mere four inches square and a restricted opening far too small for a person to get through. However, Morgan was a desperate character with ten years penal servitude ahead of him and on the day of his escape, either through negligence by or with the connivance of a warder, had smuggled the head of a sledgehammer into the prison on his return from labour.

It was a Sunday evening and suppers had just been served when Morgan literally made his 'break' by smashing through the iron framework of his cell window with the hammer head. He timed the blows to coincide with a ritual sound he'd heard hundreds of times, the rhythmical banging of cell doors by the warders (hence the term 'banged up'). The aperture he made in the limited time available to him was surprisingly small, prompting the comment that it was not the first time an escapee had demonstrated an opening large enough for the head to pass through was large enough for the body too (in 1851 a prisoner called Thomas Clutch actually slipped between the bars to freedom). Morgan had to strip in order to squeeze through the jagged opening and injured himself in the process. After throwing his clothes out he lowered himself to the ground using an improvised rope made from twisted bed sheets and climbed over the prison wall with the aid of a discarded wooden pole he found in the yard.

He afterwards admitted he had singled out a particular house he could see from his cell window on the Rundlestone – Two Bridges road which he intended breaking into for a change of clothes every escaped convict's needs. However, to his dismay the place was still lit and there was the barking of dogs on his approach, leaving him to face the rigours of the open moor in the blackness of night and the winter cold. He kept going for two nights and a day without food or drink, and bleeding from the wounds he sustained climbing out of his damaged cell window. On Tuesday he was on the upper reaches of the River Teign, close to Scorhill stone circle. He was surveying a house which he contemplated raiding after dark in the hope of finding food when he was seen by a farmer named Perryman who, observing he had no hat or coat, guessed at once who he was.

Morgan made a run for it but the farmer urged his dog after him and it clamped its jaws into Morgan's breeches, slowing him sufficiently for the farmer to catch up. The convict faced Mr. Perryman's levelled shotgun defiantly, believing it to be empty until he was shown the cartridge in the breech. That settled it. The fugitive went before his captor to the very house he had been planning to break into that night, instead of which he was the 'guest' of kindly Mr. Perryman who gave him bread and cheese and some milk before taking him to Chagford where the local Constable took charge of him.

William Morgan displayed exceptional fortitude in his unsuccessful escape bid, and he taught the prison authorities a lesson because every cell window was later fitted with bars.

A BRIEF TASTE OF FREEDOM

It was a glorious sunny day during June 1924, which attracted many visitors to Princetown. Most of them had come to see the prison and the convict working parties which were a common feature on the moor in those days. One had only to go along the Rundlestone – Two Bridges road to observe the farm parties at work and in the town itself, if you were lucky, at the right time of day you got a close up view of armed guards escorting prisoners to and from their place of work. There was a curious fascination about the prison and its inmates which persists to the present day.

Check-point on Dartmoor 1932 searching for an escaped prisoner –
Constable Sid Pollard of Tavistock with a prison warder
(Courtesy Simon Dell M.B.E., Q.C.B.)

A drama was about to be enacted which took sightseers and moor-lovers alike by surprise and gave them a tale to tell for years to come. Around 300 convicts who were haymaking in a prison farm field known as Park Corner had just stopped for a lunch break. It was a peaceful scene: the convicts sat in the shade of a stone wall eating their dinners of pea soup, potatoes and bread out of round prison dinner cans (a four-wheeled cart brought their dinners from the prison); half the number of warders in charge were also having their dinner, sitting in a group in the middle of the field whilst their comrades kept watch until their turn to eat. Suddenly there was a whistle blast sounding an alarm – seven prisoners had made a dash for freedom. Over the hedge they sped and scattered, pursued by mounted warders armed with pistols. When one of them opened fire two of the fugitives were wounded; the remaining five ran for dear life, discarding their prison issue boots with the imprint of the famous 'broad arrow' nailed into the soles which would leave an unmistakable trail to be followed. One man shed his breeches and belt as well to allow the maximum freedom of movement in his flight leaving him clad with just his shirt and underwear.

The remaining convicts formed two files and were escorted back to the prison. One warder ran to a nearby telegraph pole where there was a field telephone communicating with the watch tower adjacent to the prison quarry where watchers could observe most of the farmland. Within minutes the surrounding countryside was overrun by uniformed officers speeding to their appointed locations. They would maintain a lookout for any sign of the missing men, some with binoculars and others with firearms, all of them intent on containing the runaways within a cordon. All traffic on the moor was halted at roadblocks and the drivers questioned, in the hope they may have seen suspicious looking people during their journey and be able to pinpoint possible areas to extend the searches. A watch had to be kept also on unattended motor cars left at the roadside by picnickers, an additional task but a necessary one because all the escapees could drive. All adjacent police forces were informed of the escapes together with descriptions of the missing men and immediate assistance was given by the Plymouth City Police under Chief Constable H. Sanders who arranged for checkpoints to be established at key points around the moor. Answering questions from reporters arriving at the scene the Prison Governor, Major F. Morgan, commented: 'They are inside a ring. It is only a matter of closing in on them', adding 'we have got no lambs here, they are all old hands'. Warders engaged in the hunt were more forthright, describing three of them as highly dangerous individuals.

It was not a good day for absconding from prison. The brilliant sunshine and clear skies made for excellent visibility on Dartmoor and that, together with the large number of visitors present, some of whom enthusiastically joined in the search, meant that the convicts' time at large would be very limited. In fact for two of the men their 'liberty' lasted a mere twenty minutes. Constable Kelleway the resident Princetown policeman was informed that loud whistles (a recognised alarm signal) were heard near the Oakery, a little dell between Princetown and

Two Bridges. He at once got on his bicycle and met the warders who had seen the escapees and told him which way they had gone. At a point nearer to Two Bridges he left his bike and legged it across the moor, catching sight of two of the men almost at once heading towards Bachelors Hall. He caught up with and restrained a convict named Ray whilst the other man by the name of Cox got away by jumping over the nearby leat only to meet up with a search party and recaptured.

Already hundreds of excited sightseers had congregated in an almost festive mood, a trait most certainly not shared by prison staff faced with the responsibility of hunting the escapees. For those who were in charge of the haymaking party, there was the unpleasant prospect of disciplinary charges being brought against them for negligence. The visitors who managed to catch sight of the recaptured men described them in over-dramatised terms such as (from a motorist): 'I did not notice them very closely because I was more concerned with avoiding them – they looked very fierce', and from a bystander: 'He was a fierce-looking brute with a murderous expression'. All of which no doubt held their listeners spellbound in the days ahead.

Out on the moor the warders continued the hunt relentlessly, some on horseback others on foot, covering a wide sweep towards the Yelverton – Plymouth area where their quarry was last seen heading. At 5.00 pm their attention was drawn to a wet morass where one of the dogs accompanying them was acting in an agitated manner. On investigation they found one of the convicts immersed up to his neck in the watery mire in an attempt at concealment. He was physically weary and easily taken into custody just as his companion, who had been hiding close by tried to run off. He too was easily caught and the two men, whose names were Myers and Ford, were taken back to the prison.

It was around 7.30 pm before the fifth and last man was recaptured on the moor in the direction of Yelverton. He was called Evans and it was he who had shed his clothing as well as his boots, which was a foolish thing to do even on a Dartmoor summer day. By the time he was recaptured he was not only hungry and exhausted but was beginning to suffer from the cold that creeps over the high moorland near to dusk. He would certainly have ended up a sick man from exposure if he had not been discovered before nightfall.

It had been a day of assorted events. The seven runaways, two of whom it will be remembered were nursing wounds, learned a harsh lesson in their futile effort to escape and would be punished for their efforts. Their colleagues in the prison, who were locked up whilst the hunt was in progress, were sure to give them a hard time as a result. The warders in charge of that particular farm party awaited the reprimands that would inevitably follow an inquiry. The holidaymakers and local residents had an entertaining afternoon and the newspapers got their story.

JENNINGS'S TAXI

One of the most daring escapes in Dartmoor's history occurred when three inmates stole an oil tanker and used it as a battering ram to smash their way out of the prison. The morning of Monday 24 June 1963 started quietly enough. At 9.00 am a ten ton tanker lorry arrived to make a delivery of fuel oil to the boiler house, which is situated in the lower half of the prison's circular enclosure. Inmates on their way to exercise at 9.15 am must have noticed its arrival and departure many times, and three of them, James Henry Jennings, 27, serving 15 years for assault and robbery; Raymond Charles Matthews, 24, doing 10 years for armed robbery; and Leslie Anthony Moore, 34, serving 5 years for office breaking and robbery; all had a particular interest in the proceedings that day. Getting out of prison was on their minds, and when they acted it was so swift and sudden everyone was taken by surprise.

The driver had finished unloading and was replacing the delivery hoses when the three prisoners broke away from the exercise yard and sprinted for the tanker, brushing the driver aside and hustling the escorting officer, who tried to restrain Moore, out of their way. They climbed into the cab and the engine roared as the tanker reversed out of the unloading bay, whilst the now stranded driver and prison officer companion did the only thing they could do in an effort to stop the escapees: they picked up all the loose stones they could find and threw them at the windscreen, shattering it. This failed to deter them though, and the driver watched helplessly as his vehicle headed for the main gate. A passing workman carrying cans of paint hurled them at the windows, breaking one of them as the lorry went by, but it still didn't stop. Pandemonium ensued as more officers appeared and tried to intervene, only to be beaten off by the runaways' flailing arms, one of them wielding a large oil can and another hitting out with a metal hose key.

There was no way they could have got out via the main gate, but that was not their objective. The driver swung the wheel and the vehicle veered left past the hospital, demolishing a low wall and some railings as it did so, and picked up speed downhill in a circular path inside the boundary wall. They were making for the football pitch and a second, unmanned gate adjacent to it at the rear of the prison. This back exit led to the prison farm and comprised two sets of high double doors, one of solid wood, the other one of steel, both locked and bolted. The fugitives had made up their minds to take this way out and proceeded to do so in heroic fashion. Using the length of the pitch to gather more speed, the tanker was driven straight at the gates and there was the sound of splintered wood as the doors were torn off their hinges by the impact. Then there was a crashing of metal as the second pair of doors gave way, extensively damaging the tanker and injuring the escapees with splinters of flying glass from the windscreen and windows.

They were outside now on a rough track leading to the Rundlestone – Two Bridges road and the driver raced for the road, reaching the gate leading to it just in time for a quick thinking Moore to run out and flag down a passing car. The driver innocently stopped to ask what was wrong, only to be dragged from his vehicle by the escapees who then piled in and drove off. Someone had called out 'Don't use any violence!' and a relieved motorist found himself unharmed at the side of the road but nevertheless dismayed to see his car disappearing in the distance towards Two Bridges. Three prisoners, two of them of a violent disposition, had got clean away from the heart of Dartmoor prison in a matter of minutes and in broad daylight.

By now the alarm had been raised and soon there were police check points and search parties organised. Police with tracker dogs were sent from as far away as Honiton and Torquay to reinforce the Tavistock contingent and prison officers looking for the missing men. We do not know what Jennings and his companions intended once they were free, but having accomplished the most difficult and dangerous part of their plan, their luck ran out. The stolen car was found to be low on petrol, forcing them to do the only thing possible – look for somewhere to hide. At Postbridge they turned right towards Widecombe-in-the-Moor and drove to Soussons Common, most of which was not a common at all, but comprised over 600 acres of fir plantations. The car was concealed with branches and ferns as the runaways, knowing the police road checks would be scaled down after twenty-four hours if they weren't found, prepared to lie low.

Again luck was against them because they'd been seen entering the area by two forestry workers who, when they heard about the escape, returned and found the car under its camouflage covering. The police were alerted and by 1.00 pm they were ready to tackle the enormous task confronting them – how to flush out three desperate men hiding in a vast wood. Fortunately help was at hand; a Territorial Army unit from Kent, based at Okehampton Camp, who were exercising on the moor, willingly abandoned their 'exercises' to help with the search.

It was the 'Terriers' who had the greatest success. The Soussons Wood conifers at that time were only four to ten feet high with thick undergrowth and ferns which made the search a long and tedious affair. The area was divided into 'squares' and systematically combed by the combined forces. I took five hours to do it. Two young soldiers stumbled on Matthews who was lying concealed in the undergrowth, and despite a frantic effort to get away, during which he aimed a blow at one of them, they managed to hold him until prison officers rushed in and took him into custody. Shortly afterwards Jennings was located by police dog ' Astor', and was recaptured. Moore was the last to be caught, by another T.A. soldier. He had a weak heart and made no resistance as he was handed over to be taken back to Dartmoor. Jennings, Matthews, and Moore all appeared at Devon Assizes later that year charged with:-

1. Taking and driving away a tanker without the owner's consent.
2. Malicious damage to prison property.
3. Escaping from HM Prison (every escapee faced the magistrates on this charge at that time. Today jurisdiction is in the hands of the prison governor).

They were each found 'Guilty as charged' and sentenced to six months, nine months, and fifteen months imprisonment, to run concurrently, but to be consecutive to, the sentences already being served. It was an ignominious ending to an amazing break out. The trio have long since left the 'moor', but Jennings, who seemed to have been the ringleader, is still remembered when prison officers who served at Dartmoor get to yarning about the day three prisoners went for a ride in 'Jennings's Taxi'.

Jennings's Taxi – after the misadventure. The fugitives were caught hiding in woods near Postbridge (Author's collection)

ACKNOWLEDGEMENTS

I wish to thank Mr. John Lawrence, former Governor of Dartmoor Prison, for his generous help when preparing material for my previous two escape books.

I owe much to my many friends and former colleagues at H.M.P. Dartmoor, past and present, for their recollections and unfailing patience in answering questions. Prison Officer Mike Chamberlain (Rtd.) was more than generous as was Mr. Brett Johnson, former Curator at Dartmoor Prison Museum, and Mr. Brian Dingle the present Curator. Officers of Devon and Cornwall Constabulary, serving and retired, who have been very supportive include Superintendent D. Roper (Rtd.), the late Sergeant K. Northey (Rtd.) and especially Police Constable Simon Dell, M.B.E., Q.C.B. (Rtd.) a firm friend and kindly critic who has contributed much.

I am grateful too for the kind assistance given by the late Mr B. Estill (former Curator Devon and Cornwall Constabulary Museum) and Mr. D. German (formerly of Princetown).

Trevor James 2015

First published by Orchard in this edition 2015

Orchard is an imprint of Tor Mark,
United Downs Ind. Est., St Day, Redruth TR16 5HY

Text copyright © Trevor James 2015
Illustrations as listed in the captions. All rights reserved

ISBN 978 1 898964 93 3

Printed by Hedgerow Print, Marsh Lane, Lord's Meadow,
Crediton EX17 1ES

FRONT COVER – *H.M.P. Dartmoor, Princetown (Courtesy Stephanie Spry © 2015)*

BACK COVER – *P.C. Joe Gater (in plain clothes) searching for an escaped convict from Dartmoor Prison with the help of bloodhound 'Turpin'. The hound was regularly loaned from Mrs. H. M. Blakiston of Bratton Clovelly and later Lydford who bred them (Courtesy of Simon Dell M.B.E., Q.C.B.)*